X

W9-DFZ-299

DATE DUE

Demco, Inc. 38-293

The Science of Soil

Soil

LIVING SCIENCE

Jonathan Bocknek

Gareth Stevens Publishing
MILWAUKEE

For a free color catalog describing Gareth Stevens' list of high-quality books and multimedia programs, call 1-800-542-2595 (USA) or 1-800-461-9120 (Canada). Gareth Stevens Publishing's Fax: (414) 225-0377.

Library of Congress Cataloging-in-Publication Data

Bocknek, Jonathan.
    The science of soil / by Jonathan Bocknek.
        p. cm. — (Living science)
    Includes index.
    Summary: Discusses the sources, ingredients, types, and nutrients
of soil and the life forms that it supports.
    ISBN 0-8368-2468-7 (lib. bdg.)
    1. Soils — Juvenile literature. 2. Soil ecology — Juvenile literature.
[1. Soils. 2. Soil ecology 3. Ecology] I. Title. II. Series: Living science
(Milwaukee, Wis.)
    S591.3.B63 1999
    631.4 — dc21   99-26929

This edition first published in 1999 by
Gareth Stevens Publishing
1555 North RiverCenter Drive, Suite 201
Milwaukee, WI 53212 USA

Project Co-ordinator: Samantha McCrory
Series Editor: Leslie Strudwick
Copy Editor: Ann Sullivan
Design and Illustration: Warren Clark
Cover Design: Carole Knox
Layout: Lucinda Cage
Gareth Stevens Editor: Patricia Lantier-Sampon

Every reasonable effort has been made to trace ownership and to obtain permission to reprint
copyright material. The publishers would be pleased to have any errors or omissions brought
to their attention so that they may be corrected in subsequent printings.

Photograph Credits:
Canada in Stock/Ivy Images: page 16 (Norman Piluke); Corel Corporation: cover, pages 4, 7, 8,
9, 10 top, 10 bottom right, 11, 13, 15 top, 18, 19 bottom left, 19 bottom right, 20, 21 bottom, 26,
27, 30, 31; Paul Hickson: page 5; Ivy Images: pages 6 (Bill Ivy), 28 (Ed Lallo/Spectrum Stock),
29 (Martin Thompson/Spectrum Stock); Tom Stack & Associates: pages 21 top (Thomas Kitchin),
22 (Dominique Braud), 25 top (W. Perry Conway); J.D. Taylor: page 24; Courtesy of University
of Idaho: page 10 bottom left; Visuals Unlimited: pages 12 (C.P. Vance), 14 (William E. Grenfell Jr.),
15 bottom (Bill Beatty), 19 top (John D. Cunningham), 23 top (John S. Flannery), 23 bottom,
25 bottom (Mark A. Schneider).

Printed in Canada

1 2 3 4 5 6 7 8 9 03 02 01 00 99

Contents

What Do You Know about Soil? 4

Soil Ingredients 6

Sources of Soil 8

Soil Types 10

Animals That Live in Soil 12

Our Friend the Earthworm . 14

Soil Layers 16

Nutrients in Soil 18

The Mineral Balance 20

Flood and Drought 22

Stories in Soil 24

Building with Soil 26

Would You Like to Be an Organic Farmer? . . . 28

Soil in Danger 30

Glossary 32

Index 32

Web Sites 32

What Do You Know about Soil?

Soil is an important part of our planet. Soil is a home for plants, animals, and the tiniest living things. It can stick to your knees or jeans when you kneel in the garden. Soil provides materials to build houses and make works of art. Soil makes it possible for farmers to grow corn, apples, and all the foods we need to be healthy. Soil even keeps a diary of Earth's history so we can tell what our planet was like long ago.

Soil is under your feet on the beach.

Soil is present under the grass in a field or park. It is under the buildings in a city or town. Deserts and forests have soil, and so do mountains. When a volcano erupts, it throws smoky, dusty soil into the air. Ponds, rivers, lakes, and huge oceans contain soil.

Soil is everywhere on our planet.

The air was filled with ash when Washington state's Mount Saint Helens erupted.

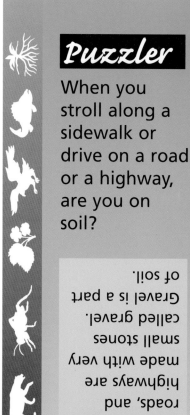

Puzzler

When you stroll along a sidewalk or drive on a road or a highway, are you on soil?

Answer: Yes. Sidewalks, roads, and highways are made with very small stones called gravel. Gravel is a part of soil.

Soil Ingredients

S oil and dirt are different substances. Dirt is something you wash from your hands and your clothes. Soil is alive. It is a mixture of living material and nonliving material.

The living material in soil is called **humus**.

Humus comes from the rotting parts of dead plants and animals.

Water, air, and bits of rock are the nonliving materials that make up soil. Half of the ingredients in soil are water and air. This is because tiny spaces exist between all the pieces of rock. The spaces are like pockets that trap water and air. Plants use the trapped water and air to grow. Air contains **oxygen**, which plants need to stay healthy. Plants make more oxygen than they need once they have green leaves.

Activity

See the Soil Ingredients

Use some water to separate the ingredients in soil.

1. Put about two tablespoons of soil in a jar.
2. Fill half the jar with water and put the lid on tightly.
3. Hold the jar in both hands and shake it to mix everything together.
4. Let the jar sit for a day.
5. Do you see the different layers? The bits of rock on the bottom are sand. The bits of rock above the sand are silt. Above them, you can see tiny, floating bits of clay. The material at the very top is humus.

Sources of Soil

The tiny pieces of rock in soil were once parts of boulders, larger rocks, or even mountains. Natural forces, such as rain, rivers, wind, and ice, can wear down and break solid rock into tiny pieces. These same forces can move the rock pieces to new places. Eventually, these pieces form soil.

Thousands of years ago, **glaciers** covered large portions of the world. As the glaciers slowly moved, they scraped the ground beneath them. Rocky soil material was left behind when the glaciers melted.

Rocks along the bottom and sides of a flowing river are worn down by moving water.

Activity

Experiment with Water and Ice

1. Spread some sand on a wooden board. Rub an ice cube back and forth along the sand. What happens to some of the sand? What happens to the board?

2. Make a sand sculpture. It can be a sand castle, a sand fortress, or even just a big mound of sand. Put some water in a small bottle or a watering can. Pour it over your sand sculpture. What do you see? What happens if you pour the water more slowly or more quickly? What happens if you pour the water from farther away or from closer?

3. Make up your own experiments to test the power of water and ice.

4. Draw or paint a picture that shows all of your new discoveries.

Soil Types

All soils are mixtures of tiny pieces of rock, water, air, and humus. Different amounts of these soil ingredients make different types of soil. Scientists **classify** soil based on the amount of sand, silt, or clay it contains. These soil ingredients help give soils their color. Usually, darker-colored soils have more humus than lighter-colored soils.

Sandy Soils

feel gritty. They do not hold water very well. Sandy soils usually have a light color.

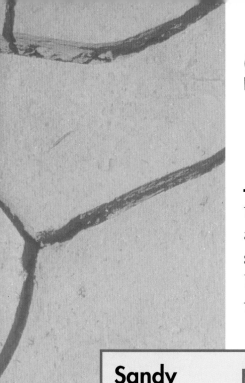

Clay Soils

feel slippery and sticky. They can hold great amounts of water. Clay soils usually have a dark brown color.

Silty Soils

feel smooth. They can hold a lot of water. Silty soils usually have a brownish color.

Which is the best soil for growing plants? That depends on the kind of plants you want to grow. Most plants grow well in soil that has equal amounts of sand, silt, and clay. This type of soil is called **loam**. Loam is good for growing plants because it has the right amount of humus and water to keep plants healthy.

Activity

Test Soil Texture

Texture is the way something feels. Make some mud balls to test the texture of the soil where you live.

1. Put a spoonful of soil in your hand.
2. Add enough water to make it wet, but not soaked.
3. Try rolling the wet soil into the shape of a ball.
4. If your mud ball feels gritty and will not hold together well, it is made of sandy soil. If it feels slick and slippery, and holds together well, it is made of clay soil. If it feels a bit slippery but falls apart fairly easily, it is made of silty soil.
5. What type is your soil? Is the soil in other parts of your neighborhood the same? Try the soil texture test to find out.

Animals That Live in Soil

Millions of living things make their homes in soil. Some live in the soil for a short time to stay cool or to keep safe from **predators**. Others live in the soil all year long. Most of these full-time dwellers are so tiny you need a **microscope** to see them. They are called **bacteria**.

Bacteria are tiny **decomposers**. There might be millions of bacteria in only a handful of soil. Bacteria make soil fertile, because they produce most of the humus in soil.

As bacteria digest food, they release **nutrients** back into the soil. Plants need these nutrients to grow.

Burrowing animals dig holes and tunnels that bring air and water into the soil. Ants, bees, birds, gophers, moles, snails, toads, turtles, and worms are expert burrowers.

Mushrooms also help make soil fertile. Like bacteria, they use dead plants and animals for food, and they release nutrients back into the soil.

Puzzler

If you were a burrowing animal, what skills and body parts would you want to have?

Answer: You might borrow some skills and body parts from some of nature's best burrowers. For example, moles have powerful arms and long, sharp claws for digging. Gophers and chipmunks are fast and full of energy, so they can dig for a long time without getting tired. Ants are very strong. They can lift sand grains and pebbles that are much heavier than they are.

Our Friend the Earthworm

Earthworms help soil in many ways. In their search for food, they eat dead and rotting plant material. Their wastes are rich in nutrients, which plants use to grow. Earthworms are also super burrowers. The tunnels they make as they slither through the soil let air and water come inside. Plants and other soil dwellers need the air and water, too.

When it rains, earthworms must come to the soil surface or they will drown.

Farmers and gardeners use earthworms to help them determine the health of their soil. Earthworms that live in fertile soil are usually dark colored. If the soil has too much water or not enough nutrients, the earthworms are usually pale.

Earthworms keep the soil healthy so plants grow better.

Puzzler

How can you tell which end of an earthworm is the front end?

Answer:
One end of an earthworm has a small piece that looks like a tiny knob. That is the front end.

Soil Layers

Soil forms in layers. You can see these layers when bulldozers dig deep into the ground for new building projects.

Workers use mining equipment to dig large pits. Mines provide mineral substances for making airplanes, refrigerators, jewelry, and other products.

Topsoil is the first soil layer. It is very fertile because it usually has a lot of humus.

Subsoil is the second soil layer, beneath the topsoil. Subsoil has a lighter color than topsoil because it has less humus. It is also packed more tightly, so there are fewer spaces to trap air and water.

Parent material is the third soil layer, beneath the subsoil. It is often the place that creates topsoil and subsoil. Parent material is made up of rocks, gravel, sand, and clay. There is no humus in this layer of soil.

Bedrock is the fourth soil layer, beneath the parent material. Bedrock is solid rock.

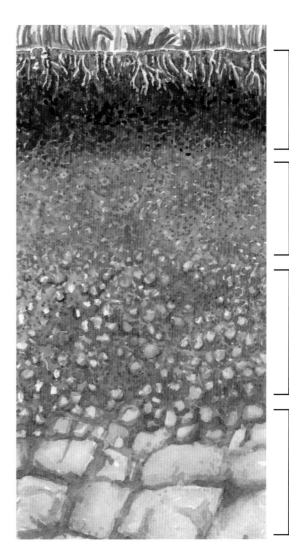

topsoil

subsoil

parent material

bedrock

Puzzler

Which soil layer do you think has the most living things?

Answer:
Topsoil has the most living things. Topsoil is the layer in which the plants we depend on grow. Also, the humus in topsoil means there must be many living things that are active in this layer.

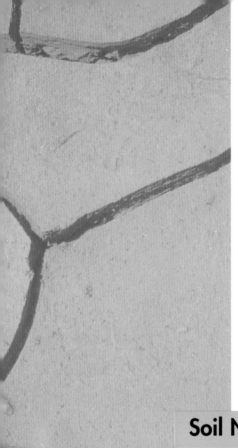

Nutrients in Soil

People depend on plants for food and oxygen. Certain plants, such as trees, are used to build homes. Soil is important because plants use it to grow and stay healthy.

Soil contains nutrients called minerals. Plants need only small amounts of these minerals. If they get too much, they can die. If they do not get enough, they cannot grow properly. Minerals come from two soil ingredients. They come from the tiny pieces of rock and the humus.

Soil Nutrient

Nitrogen	Phosphorous	Potassium

What does it do?

Nitrogen	Phosphorous	Potassium
• helps plants grow • helps plants stay green	• helps form flowers, fruits, and seeds • helps roots grow	• helps plants resist diseases • makes seeds healthier

Manure is a good source of nitrogen.

Farmers and gardeners help keep soils fertile by adding **fertilizers**. Some fertilizers come from nature. For example, plants and animals add nutrients, such as calcium and nitrogen, to the soil. Other fertilizers are made in factories.

Calcium	Magnesium
• helps plants absorb other nutrients they need • helps roots and leaves grow	• helps plants use sunlight to make food, because magnesium is a key part of **chlorophyll**

Activity

Do Your Own Research
Visit a library and try to find the answers to these questions:

• Why do some soils become less fertile?
• How does adding fertilizer help?
• What else can we add to soils to give them more nutrients?

The Mineral Balance

By late spring, most plants are on their way to a new year of growth. Some plants may be shorter than they should be or have yellowing leaves. This can happen if they do not have enough water. It can also happen if the soil is too **alkaline**. This means that the soil contains too many minerals, such as calcium and salt.

Desert soil is alkaline. Cactus plants grow best in this kind of soil.

The opposite of alkaline soil is **acidic** soil. Acidic soil does not have enough minerals, such as calcium and magnesium.

Blueberries are one of the few plants that can grow well in acidic soil.

Many vegetables grow best in soil that is between acidic and alkaline, or that is slightly acidic.

Puzzler

Why would farmers and gardeners want to know if their soil is acidic or alkaline?

Answer: Knowing if the soil is acidic or alkaline helps farmers and gardeners know what kinds of crops will grow best. It also helps them decide whether they need to treat their soil to make it healthier for growing the kinds of plants they want.

Flood and Drought

Some of the best places to grow food plants are in flat parts of the world called **floodplains**. The North American prairies and Egypt's Nile Valley are two such places.

The rivers that flow through these areas often rise above their banks. The nutrients in the river water help make the soil more fertile. People set up houses and farms in floodplains because the soil is very good for growing food plants.

Sometimes, heavy rains or melting snow quickly add too much water to the rivers. When the water rises over the riverbanks, flooding causes great damage. Houses are destroyed, and many people have to flee as the water gets deeper. Too much flooding can strip valuable topsoil from the land and wash it away.

In 1997, many towns were flooded in the Red River Valley area of the midwestern United States and Canada.

While too much water is not good for soils, too little water is not good, either. **Drought** causes topsoil to dry out and become crumbly and dusty. Winds easily blow the dusty soil away.

Drought causes serious damage to farmers' crops.

In the 1930s, a severe drought parched the soil on the North American prairies. Windstorms pounded the area for several years.

Activity

Do Some Research at the Library or on the Internet

- Look up the term *Dust Bowl* to find out about the windstorms that destroyed the North American prairies.
- Look up the term *Red River* to find out about the flooding that occurred in parts of Canada and the United States in 1997.
- Look up the term *Nile River* to find out about the history of Egypt's most important waterway.

Stories in Soil

Have you ever visited a museum to see dinosaur bones and **fossils**? Fossils form in soil material that has hardened to become solid rock.

When an ancient animal died and was covered with layers of soil, it became a cast fossil.

Scientists are interested in fossils because fossils can tell a great deal about what life was like in the past. For example, many plants and animals that lived long ago are now **extinct**. They are not alive anywhere on Earth. Their footprints, outlines, and body parts are like stories that have hardened in soil. Scientists know how to read these stories.

An imprint or impression in soil can become a mold fossil. Dinosaur footprints and leaf imprints are examples of mold fossils.

Make a Mold Fossil

1. Put some thick mud in a small plastic cup. If you cannot get or make any mud, you can use modeling clay or a fast-hardening product called Plaster of Paris.
2. Make the top of the mud smooth.
3. Press a shell or coin into the mud. Take out the shell or coin and let the mud harden. You have just made a mold fossil!

Make a Cast Fossil

1. Push the whole shell or coin into the mud so it is covered. Let the mud harden. When you peel off the plastic cup, you have your very own self-made rock. Inside is a cast fossil!
2. Show your rock to friends and family members. Let them figure out how to discover the fossil you have made.

Building with Soil

Cement is an important product in our modern world. Cement is used to hold houses and buildings together. Workers also use cement to make streets and sidewalks. Cement comes from soil.

Cement has many different uses. It can glue bricks together or make strong columns to support buildings.

Cement is a gray-colored powder made from clay, sand, and finely crushed rocks. When cement is mixed with water, sand, and gravel, the result is a thick, wet material that is similar to heavy modeling clay. This material hardens to form a useful building material called concrete.

Cement is used to make concrete sidewalks.

Adobe homes are made from mud mixed with straw and grasses.

Puzzler

Is there anywhere on Earth that you can go and not be on soil or something made with soil?

Answer: Unless you are flying in an airplane or a hot-air balloon, you probably cannot escape soil. Whenever your feet are on the ground, you are on soil or something made with soil. If you are in a boat, you are on water. However, what is at the bottom of the water? Soil!

27

Would You Like to Be an Organic Farmer?

Organic farmers grow plants in the most natural way possible. This means they treat their soil and crops in special ways. They use manure and plant wastes to fertilize their soil instead of factory-made fertilizers. They also leave the roots and stems of harvested crops in the ground during winter. As they rot, the roots and stems add nutrients to the soil to help it stay fertile and healthy.

Greenhouses protect plants from harmful insects and bad weather.

Organic farmers do not use chemical pesticides (poisons) to kill insects and other plant pests that harm their crops. Instead, they pick out the insects by hand, or they grow other kinds of plants that the insects do not like.

Being an organic farmer is a hard life, but a satisfying one. Would you like to be an organic farmer? Find out more about organic farming to help you decide.

Activity

Do Your Own Research
Ask a parent or teacher to help you find information about these soil careers:

- farmer
- forester
- landscape architect
- sculptor
- seedling grower
- soil scientist

Soil in Danger

Soil is everywhere on our planet. Most living things depend on soil for food and shelter. Of all the soil in the world, only a small portion is best for growing food. Most of this soil needs special care from people to keep it fertile for long-term use.

The human population gets larger every day. More and more space is necessary for everyone to live. Often, this means moving onto soil that is best suited for growing food. The land people live on is also home to many kinds of plants and animals.

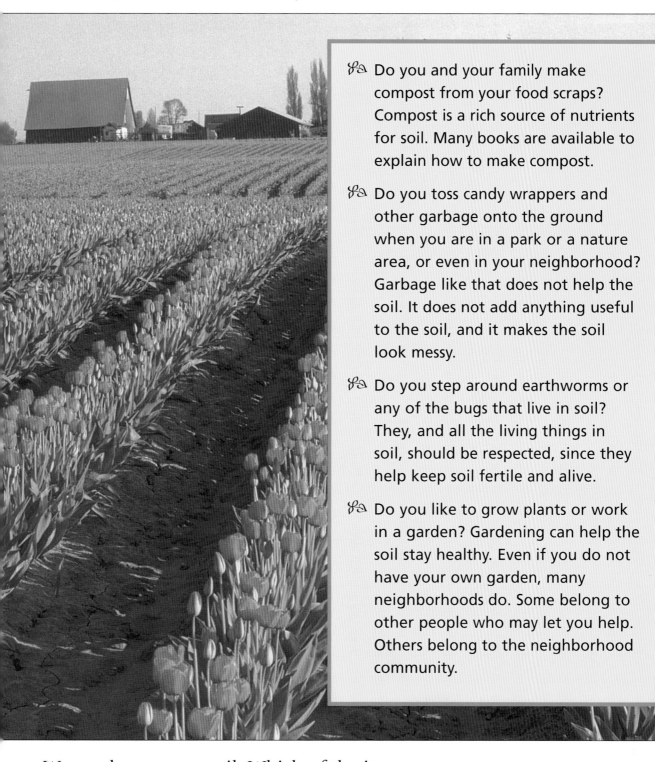

Do you and your family make compost from your food scraps? Compost is a rich source of nutrients for soil. Many books are available to explain how to make compost.

Do you toss candy wrappers and other garbage onto the ground when you are in a park or a nature area, or even in your neighborhood? Garbage like that does not help the soil. It does not add anything useful to the soil, and it makes the soil look messy.

Do you step around earthworms or any of the bugs that live in soil? They, and all the living things in soil, should be respected, since they help keep soil fertile and alive.

Do you like to grow plants or work in a garden? Gardening can help the soil stay healthy. Even if you do not have your own garden, many neighborhoods do. Some belong to other people who may let you help. Others belong to the neighborhood community.

We need to protect soil. Which of the items on this checklist do you do now? Which ones would you like to start doing?

Glossary

acidic soil: soil with not enough minerals in it.

alkaline soil: soil with too many minerals in it.

bacteria: tiny one-celled living organisms.

chlorophyll: a green substance that plants use to make food.

classify: to arrange things into groups by comparing how they are alike.

decomposers: living things, such as bacteria and mushrooms, that digest the remains of dead plants and animals.

drought: when there is no rain in an area for a long period of time.

extinct: no longer in existence.

fertilizer: a chemical that adds nutrients to the soil.

floodplain: the flat land on both sides of a river or stream.

fossils: the body parts and shapes of living and nonliving things that are preserved in rock.

glaciers: slow-moving masses of ice.

humus: the living material in soil.

loam: a type of soil made up of equal amounts of sand, silt, and clay.

microscope: a viewing instrument that makes very tiny things appear much larger.

nutrients: substances that provide nourishment.

oxygen: a gas found in air that plants and animals need to survive.

predators: animals that eat other animals for food.

Index

acidic 21
adobe 27
alkaline 20, 21

bacteria 12, 13
bedrock 17
burrow 13, 14

calcium 19, 20, 21
cement 26, 27
chlorophyll 19
classify 10
clay 7, 10, 11, 17, 25, 27
concrete 27

decomposers 12
dirt 6
drought 22, 23

earthworms 14, 15, 31
extinct 25

fertile 12, 13, 15, 17, 19, 22, 28, 30, 31
fertilizer 19, 28
flood 22, 23
floodplain 22
fossils 24, 25

glaciers 8
gravel 5, 17, 27

humus 6, 7, 10, 11, 12, 17, 18

ice 8, 9

loam 11

magnesium 19, 21
microscope 12
minerals 18, 20, 21
mushrooms 13

nitrogen 18, 19
nutrients 12, 13, 14, 15, 18, 19, 22, 28, 31

organic 28, 29
oxygen 7, 18

parent material 17
pesticides 29
phosphorous 18
potassium 18
predators 12

sand 7, 9, 10, 11, 13, 17, 27
silt 7, 10, 11
subsoil 17

texture 11
topsoil 17, 22, 23

Web Sites

www.arnprior.com/kidsgarden/index.htm

ltpwww.gsfc.nasa.gov/globe/index.htm

www.planet.com/dirtweb/dirt.html

www.osweb.com/kidzkorner/rocknroll.htm

Some web sites stay current longer than others. For further web sites, use your search engines to locate the following topics: *dirt, drought, fertilizers, gravel, humus,* and *soil.*